Life in the UK Test: Questions and Answers

Valid for tests taken from April 2007

EMMANUEL ALUKO

ISBN 978-1-84799-135-5

ISBN 978-1-84799-135-5

PREFACE

Becoming a British citizen, or achieving permanent residence status in the United Kingdom, is a life changing event. New immigration rules require that migrants who want to become citizens by naturalization or who apply for indefinite leave to remain are required to demonstrate understanding of living in the UK and knowledge of the English Language. This has resulted in the introduction of the **Life in the UK test.**

This question and answer guide has been produced in order to make taking the test a lot easier, by providing 380 questions that cover most of the material you are required to understand. It is based on the second edition of the official publication from the Home Office, valid for tests from April 2007. We recommend that you use this book alongside the second edition of the official publication, as the answers have been referenced to paragraphs in the second edition book to enhance your preparedness for the test. The questions are based on guidelines of what you need to understand from the second edition book, and from the Life in the UK test website at http://www.lifeintheuktest.gov.uk/htmlsite/self_10.html. The test is based on chapters 2, 3, 4, 5 and 6 of the book, and the question and answer guide is based on these five chapters as well.

For further information about the test, we advise you to visit the Life in the UK test website at http://www.lifeintheuktest.gov.uk/htmlsite/index.html which contains further information about the test, test centre registration and what you need to know (the basis for this publication). As the test currently stands, you are required to answer 24 questions in 45 minutes through a computer based test.

You may also be using this question and answer guide to expand your understanding of how the UK works. We have endeavoured to make it comprehensive, without making it daunting. We wish you success if you are taking the test, and believe that with proper use of this question and answer guide, you will be able to pass the test the first time, and achieve a key requirement for naturalization or British Citizenship.

Contents

PREFACE 3

Chapter 1 How to use this book and what you need to know 5

Chapter 2 Questions 11

    A CHANGING SOCIETY 12

    UK TODAY: A PROFILE.. 18

    HOW THE UNITED KINGDOM IS GOVERNED 24

    EVERYDAY NEEDS... 32

    EMPLOYMENT 51

Chapter 3 Answers with book* paragraph reference 62

    A CHANGING SOCIETY 63

    UK TODAY: A PROFILE.. 65

    HOW THE UNITED KINGDOM IS GOVERNED 67

    EVERYDAY NEEDS... 70

    EMPLOYMENT 76

*LIFE IN THE UNITED KINGDOM – A journey to Citizenship Second edition ISBN-978-0-11-341313-3

Chapter 1 How to use this book and what you need to know

This question and answer book has been prepared to enable you test your understanding of the material required to pass the Life in the UK test. Current Immigration rules require that all who want to become British permanent residents or British citizens take the test to demonstrate their knowledge of life in the UK, or go for combined citizenship and language classes. The current reading material is the second edition book, 'LIFE IN THE UNITED KINGDOM – A Journey to Citizenship' from the Home Office and is valid for tests taken from April 2007.

The questions are based on guidelines on what you are advised to understand throughout the relevant chapters of the book, which are chapters 2,3,4,5 and 6. A list according to chapters is provided below. In addition, the answers are referenced to paragraphs and page numbers in the Home Office official book, to enable you further your understanding by reading the sections relevant to the questions in the book. Although it is possible to use this book standalone, it is recommended that this book is used with the official guide. The official guide can be purchased from The Stationery Office at http://www.tsoshop.co.uk/ .

What you need to know

A CHANGING SOCIETY

- ✓ Some of the historical reasons for immigration to the UK

- ✓ Some of the reasons for immigration to the UK since 1945

- ✓ The main immigrant groups coming to the UK since 1945, the countries they came from and kind of work they did

- ✓ When women aged over 30 were first given the right to vote

- ✓ When women were given equal voting rights with men

- ✓ Some of the important developments to create equal rights in the workplace

- ✓ The proportion of all young people who go on to higher education

- ✓ Lifestyle patterns of children and young people (e.g. pocket money, leaving home on reaching adulthood)

- ✓ Changing family patterns and attitudes to changing family patterns (e.g. divorce)

- ✓ That education in Britain is free and compulsory, and that there is compulsory testing (in England and Scotland) at ages 7,11 and 14; there are also GCSE and/or vocational exams at 16; and Advanced level exams (A and AS) at ages 17 and 18

- ✓ That there is a government target that half of all young people attend higher education

- ✓ That there are strict laws regarding the employment of children

- ✓ That there are important health concerns and laws relating to children and young people and smoking, alcohol and drugs

- ✓ That young people are eligible to vote in elections from age 18

UK TODAY: A PROFILE

- ✓ The size of the current UK population

- ✓ The population of Scotland, Wales and Northern Ireland

- ✓ What the census is and when the next one will be

- ✓ What the largest ethnic minorities in the UK are

- ✓ Where the largest ethnic minority people live

- ✓ What languages other than English are spoken in Wales, Scotland and Northern Ireland

- ✓ Some of the ways you can identify regional differences in the UK

- ✓ The percentage (%) of the UK population who say they are Christian

- ✓ How many people say they have no religion

- ✓ What percentage are Muslim, Hindu, Sikh, Jewish and Buddhist

- ✓ Everyone in the UK has the right to practise their religion

- ✓ The Anglican Church, or Church of England, is the church of the state in England (established church)

- ✓ The monarch (king or queen) is head of the Church of England

- ✓ In Scotland the established church is the Presbyterian Church of Scotland. In Wales and Northern Ireland there is no established church

- ✓ Which sports are most popular in the UK

- ✓ The patron saints' days in England, Scotland, Wales and Northern Ireland

- ✓ What Bank Holidays are

- ✓ The main traditional festivals in the UK

- ✓ That the main festivals in the UK are Christian based, but that important festivals from other religions are recognised and explained to children in schools.

HOW THE UNITED KINGDOM IS GOVERNED

- ✓ The role of the monarchy

- ✓ How Parliament works, and the difference between the House of Commons and the House of Lords

- ✓ How often general elections are held

- ✓ Where the official residence of the Prime Minister is

- ✓ The role of the Cabinet and who is in it

- ✓ The nature of the UK Constitution

- ✓ The job of the Opposition, the leader of the Opposition and the Shadow Cabinet

- ✓ The difference between 'first past the post' and proportional representation

- ✓ The form of electoral systems in the devolved administrations in Northern Ireland, Scotland and Wales

- ✓ The rights and duties of British Citizens, including naturalized citizens

- ✓ How the judiciary, police and local authorities work

- ✓ What non-departmental public bodies are

- ✓ The differences between the Council of Europe, the European Union, the European Commission and the European Parliament

- ✓ The UK is a member of the Council of Europe and the European Union

- ✓ The EU aims to become a single market and it is administered by a Council of Ministers of governments of member states

- ✓ Subject to some restrictions, EU citizens may travel to and work in any EU country

- ✓ The roles of the UN and the Commonwealth

EVERYDAY NEEDS

- ✓ The process for buying and renting accommodation

- ✓ Where to get advice about accommodation and moving

- ✓ The role of an estate agent

- ✓ Housing priorities for local authorities

- ✓ Where to get help if you are homeless

- ✓ How you can pay for water you use at home

- ✓ Recycling your waste

- ✓ What Council Tax pays for

- ✓ What to do if you have problems with your neighbours

✓ What you need to open a bank or building society account

✓ What debit, credit and store cards are

✓ What a credit union is

✓ What insurance is

✓ How to get help with benefits and problems with debt

✓ How to find and register with a GP

✓ What to do if you feel unwell

✓ How to find other services such as dentists and opticians

✓ When it is possible to attend A & E without a doctor's letter

✓ Who can get free prescriptions

✓ When you should phone 999 or 112

✓ What NHS Direct can do

✓ Who can give health advice and treatment when you are pregnant and after you have a baby

✓ How to register a birth

✓ The different stages of a child's education

✓ That there are differences in the education systems in England, Scotland, Wales and Northern Ireland

✓ That there are different kinds of schools, and that some of them charge fees

✓ What the National Curriculum is

✓ What the governing body of a school does

✓ Options for young people at the age of 16

✓ Course available at FE colleges

✓ Where you can get English classes or other education for adults, including university

✓ How films are classified

✓ Why you need a television licence

✓ The rules about selling and drinking of alcohol

✓ How to get a driving licence

✓ What you need to do to be allowed to drive a vehicle in the UK

✓ What you should do if you have an accident

✓ When you might have to prove your identity, and how you can do it

EMPLOYMENT

✓ The Home office provides guidance on who is entitled to work in the UK

✓ NARIC can advise on how qualifications from overseas compare with qualifications from the UK

✓ What CVs are

✓ Who can be a referee

✓ What happens if any of the information you have given is untrue

✓ When you need a CRB check

✓ Where you can find out about training opportunities and job seeking

✓ Benefits of volunteering in terms of work experience and community involvement

✓ Equal rights

- The categories covered by the law and exceptions

- Equal job/equal pay regardless of gender

- The different commissions working to promote equal opportunities

- The grounds for sexual harassment complaints

✓ At work

- The importance of contracts of employment

- The minimum wage and holiday entitlement

- Information that has to be provided on pay slips

✓ Tax

- What is deducted from your earnings and why

- The difference between self-employment and employed

- Where to get help if you need it when filling forms

- The purpose of National Insurance and what happens if you don't pay enough contributions

- How you can get a National Insurance number

✓ Pensions

- Who is entitled to a pension

- What age men and women can get a pension

-

✓ Health and Safety

- Employer and employee obligations

- What to do if you have concerns about health and safety

✓ Trade unions

- What they are and who can join

✓ Losing your job

- Where to go if you need advice on a problem at work

- Possible reasons for dismissal

- The role of Employment Tribunals

- Who can help

- The timescale for complaining

- Entitlement to redundancy pay

✓ Self-employment

- Responsibility for keeping detailed records and paying tax and national insurance

- The role of Business Link

✓ Maternity and paternity rights

- Entitlement to maternity leave and pay for both part-time and full-time workers

- Paternity leave entitlement

- The importance of following the right procedures and providing sufficient notice

✓ Children at work

- Minimum age for starting work

- Jobs 14 to 16 year olds are not allowed to do

- The maximum hours allowed

- Requirements – medical certificate and employment card

- The local authority's responsibility for protecting children

Chapter 2 Questions

A CHANGING SOCIETY

Q1. Immigration to the United Kingdom started

    A. In 1945
    B. In 1980
    C. In 1950s
    D. Before 1945

Q2. Women in Britain Make up what percentage of the UK population

    A. 49%
    B. 50%
    C. 51%
    D. 52%

Q3. There are more men than women in University

    A. True
    B. False

Q4. In the late 1960s, new laws were passed to restrict immigration to Britain and this reduced immigration from

    A. Australia
    B. India
    C. New Zealand
    D. Canada

Q5. In the late 1980s, the largest immigrant groups came from

    A. United States, India, Pakistan and Australia
    B. India, Pakistan, Australia and New Zealand
    C. United States, Australia, South Africa and New Zealand
    D. India, West Indies, Pakistan and Australia

Q6. Since 1994, there has been a global rise in migration for political and economic reasons

    A. True
    B. False

Q7. Women earned the right to divorce their husbands in

    A. 1922
    B. 1857
    C. 1882
    D. 1918

Q8. Until which year were the earnings, property and money of a married woman automatically the belongings of her husband?

        A. 1922
        B. 1857
        C. 1882
        D. 1918

Q9. 'Suffragettes' are women who fought in world war 1

        A. True
        B. False

Q10. In which year were women over the age of 30 given the right to vote?

        A. 1922
        B. 1926
        C. 1928
        D. 1918

Q11. In which year did women win the right to vote at the same age as men?

        A. 1922
        B. 1926
        C. 1928
        D. 1918

Q12. When women first got the right to vote at the same age as men, the voting age was 18.

        A. True
        B. False

Q13. It is legal in the UK to pay a woman less than a man solely based on gender

        A. True
        B. False

Q14. What percentage of the workforce is made up of women in Britain today?

        A. 43%
        B. 44%
        C. 45%
        D. 46%

Q15. Employment opportunities for women are much greater now than in the past

        A. True
        B. False

Q16. The difference between average hourly pay rate of men and women in Britain today is about

        A. 5%
        B. 10%
        C. 15%
        D. 20%

Q17. The UK has laws to prevent discrimination against women

        A. True
        B. False

Q18. The UK has about how many young people up to the age of 19

        A. 10 million
        B. 12 million
        C. 15 million
        D. 17 million

Q19. What percentage of children live in lone-parent families?

        A. 10%
        B. 20%
        C. 15%
        D. 25%

Q20. Children in the UK play outside the home just as much as they did in the past

        A. True
        B. False

Q21. By law, school is compulsory for children between the ages of

        A. 4 and 17
        B. 3 and 15
        C. 5 and 16
        D. 6 and 17

Q22. Some children in the UK get pocket money for doing jobs around the house

        A. True
        B. False

Q23. Young people typically stay within the family home when they have become adults

        A. True
        B. False

Q24. The percentage of women with school-age children who are in paid work in Britain is

     A. 25%
     B. 50%
     C. 75%
     D. 100%

Q25. Women are mainly responsible for childcare and housework in the UK today

     A. True
     B. False

Q26. In England and Scotland, Children are nationally tested at which ages?

     A. 5, 7 and 9
     B. 7, 11 and 14
     C. 7, 10 and 16
     D. 5, 9 and 15

Q27. In Wales, children are nationally tested at age 7?

     A. True
     B. False

Q28. What proportion of young people go on to higher education (college or university)?

     A. 1 in 2
     B. 2 in 3
     C. 1 in 4
     D. 1 in 3

Q29. AS and A levels exams are typically taken at what ages?

     A. 16 and 17
     B. 17 and 18
     C. 15 and 16
     D. 18 and 19

Q30 AGCE refers to

     A. General certificate of Education at an advanced vocational level
     B. General certificate of Education at an advanced subsidiary level
     C. General certificate of Education at a advanced higher level
     D. General certificate of Education at an advanced level

Q31. Young people in Britain do not work in order to save for higher education since it is free

     A. True
     B. False

Q32. The most common types of jobs done by children include

    A. Car washing and newspaper delivery
    B. Household chores and childminding
    C. Work in supermarkets and newsagents
    D. Working in a sandwich shop and retailing

Q33. There are no laws about children working in the UK

    A. True
    B. False

Q34. Smoking is illegal in the UK?

    A. True
    B. False

Q35. Which of the following statements is true about smoking in the UK?

    A. Smoking has increased for both adults and young people
    B. Smoking has increased for adults, but has decreased for young people
    C. Smoking has decreased for adults, but has increased for young people
    D. Smoking has decreased for both adults and young people

Q36. Who smokes more in the UK, boys or girls?

    A. Boys
    B. Girls
    C. No difference between boys and girls
    D. Boys and girls do not smoke at all

Q37. It is illegal to sell tobacco products to anyone under

    A. 15 years old
    B. 16 years old
    C. 17 years old
    D. 18 years old

Q38. It is illegal to sell alcohol to anyone under

    A. 15 years old
    B. 16 years old
    C. 17 years old
    D. 18 years old

Q39. What percentage of children live within a step-family?

    A. 10%
    B. 12%
    C. 15%
    D. 20%

Q40. 'Binge drinking' refers to

    A. Drinking by young people who are underage
    B. Drinking by young people in a pub
    C. Drinking a lot of alcohol at a time
    D. Drinking small amounts of alcohol

Q41. A 'gap year' refers to

    A. Time spent during A levels
    B. The year a young person enters university
    C. Deferring university entrance by a year
    D. Travelling for a year by anybody

Q42. Which TWO of the following are illegal drugs?

    A. Heroin
    B. Tobacco
    C. Cannabis
    D. Paracetamol

Q43. There is a strong link between use of hard drugs and crime?

    A. True
    B. False

Q44. What proportion of young adults has used illegal drugs at one time or the other?

    A. 30%
    B. 40%
    C. 50%
    D. 60%

Q45. Which of the following statements is correct?

    A. Drugs misuse is a serious issue for British society
    B. Drugs misuse is no longer a problem for British society

Q46. Young people in Britain can vote from what age?

    A. 16
    B. 17
    C. 18
    D. 19

Q47. The participation rate of first time voters in the 2001 general election was

    A. 1 in 2
    B. 1 in 3
    C. 1 in 4
    D. 1 in 5

Q48. Which of the following statements is correct?

    A. Young people have little interest in party politics
    B. Young people have a lot of interest in party politics

Q49. Which of the following was not amongst the five most important issues identified by young people in a 2003 survey?

    A. Immigration
    B. Crime
    C. Drugs
    D. Racism
    E. Health

Q50. Young people in Britain take part in community events including raising money for charity

    A. True
    B. False

UK TODAY: A PROFILE

Q1. The UK population in 2005 was just under

    A. 55 million people
    B. 58 million people
    C. 60 million people
    D. 62 million people

Q2. Which of the following statements is correct?

    A. In 2005, the population in England was 50.1 million, Scotland 5.1 million, Wales 2.9 million and Northern Ireland 1.7m
    B. In 2005, the population in England was 50.1 million, Scotland 2.9 million, Wales 1.7 million and Northern Ireland 5.1m

Q3. A census is carried out every 8 years

    A. True
    B. False

Q4. The next census will take place in

    A. 2010
    B. 2011
    C. 2012
    D. 2013

Q5. Which of the following statements is correct?

      A. A census is a count of those eligible to vote
      B. A census is a count of the total population

Q6. Which of the following statements is correct?

      A. The birth rate in the UK is rising, while the death rate is falling
      B. Both the birth rate and death rate in the UK is falling

Q7. Census information is collected by sending a form to:

      A. a sample of UK households
      B. to half of UK households
      C. to all UK households
      D. to a quarter of UK households

Q8. It is optional to complete a census form delivered to your household

      A. True
      B. False

Q9. Which of the following statements is correct?

      A. Ethnic minority groups make up 10.2% of the population
      B. Ethnic minority groups make up 8.3% of the population

Q10. A few citizens of the new East European states have arrived in the UK since 2004?

      A. True
      B. False

Q11. Most members of Ethnic minority groups in the UK live in:

      A. England
      B. Wales
      C. Northern Ireland
      D. Scotland

Q12. The percentage of all ethnic minority people that live in the London area is:

      A. 25%
      B. 35%
      C. 45%
      D. 55%

Q13. Ethnic minority people make up approximately what proportion of the London area population:

      A. One-half
      B. One-third
      C. One-fourth
      D. One-fifth

Q14. The largest ethnic minority group in the UK are:

    A. Black Caribbean
    B. Indian
    C. Black African
    D. Pakistani

Q15. Which of these areas does not have a large ethnic minority population?

    A. West Midlands
    B. Yorkshire and Humberside
    C. North East
    D. North West

Q16. The longest distance between two points on the British mainland is:

    A. 570 miles
    B. 680 miles
    C. 780 miles
    D. 870 miles

Q17. Which of the following statements is true?

    A. The only language spoken in the United Kingdom is English
    B. English is one of many languages spoken in the United Kingdom

Q18. Fill the blanks: Cockney is spoken in__________, Scouse in ___________ and Geordie in _________

    A. Liverpool, London, Tyneside
    B. London, Tyneside, Liverpool
    C. Liverpool, Tyneside, London
    D. London, Liverpool , Tyneside

Q19. Which of the following statements is true?

    A. Welsh is spoken in Wales, Gaelic in Scotland and Irish Gaelic in Northern Ireland
    B. Welsh is spoken in Scotland, Gaelic in Northern Island and Ulster Scots in Scotland.

Q20. The English language has many accents and dialects.

    A. True
    B. False

Q21. The percentage of the UK population that is Christian is close to:

    A. 60%
    B. 65%
    C. 70%
    D. 75%

Q22. The percentage of the UK population that say they have no religion is close to:

    A. 10%
    B. 15%
    C. 20%
    D. 25%

Q23. The head or Supreme Governor of the Church of England is the:

    A. Prime Minister
    B. King or Queen
    C. The Archbishop of Canterbury
    D. Chancellor of the Exchequer

Q24. Which of the following statements is true?

    A. The Monarch is allowed to marry anyone
    B. The Monarch is only allowed to marry a Protestant

Q25. Which of the following statements is true?

    A. The Church of England is the official church in England, the Presbyterian Church is the official church in Scotland, Wales and Northern Ireland
    B. The Church of England is the official church in England, the Presbyterian Church is the official church in Scotland and Wales and Northern Ireland have no official church

Q26. The percentage of the population who attend religious services is close to:

    A. 5%
    B. 10%
    C. 15%
    D. 20%

Q27. Rank the major UK religions in descending order of percentage of the population:

    A. Christian, Hindu, Muslim, Jewish, Buddhist and Sikh
    B. Christian, Buddhist, Sikh, Hindu, Muslim and Jewish
    C. Christian, Muslim, Hindu, Sikh, Jewish and Buddhist
    D. Christian, Jewish, Muslim, Hindu, Sikh and Buddhist

Q28. Christian groups include the Baptists, Presbyterians, Methodists and Quakers

    A. True
    B. False

Q29. Which of the following statements is true?

    A. In the UK, 40% of Christians are Roman Catholic (10% in Northern Ireland)
    B. In the UK, 10% of Christians are Roman Catholic (40% in Northern Ireland)

Q30. Bank holidays are religious public holidays

    A. True
    B. False

Q31. The patron saint day in England is:

    A. 1 March (St David's day)
    B. 17 March (St Patrick's day)
    C. 23 April (St George's day)
    D. 30 November (St Andrew's day)

Q32. The patron saint day in Wales is:

    A. 1 March (St David's day)
    B. 17 March (St Patrick's day)
    C. 23 April (St George's day)
    D. 30 November (St Andrew's day)

Q33. The patron saint day in Scotland is:

    A. 1 March (St David's day)
    B. 17 March (St Patrick's day)
    C. 23 April (St George's day)
    D. 30 November (St Andrew's day)

Q34. The patron saint day in Northern Ireland is:

    A. 1 March (St David's day)
    B. 17 March (St Patrick's day)
    C. 23 April (St George's day)
    D. 30 November (St Andrew's day)

Q35. Boxing Day is:

    A. January 1
    B. December 31
    C. December 24
    D. December 26

Q36. Hogmanay is a holiday in Scotland and is on December 31

    A. True
    B. False

Q37. Which of the following statements is true?

    A. Customs and traditions from various religions are celebrated in the UK
    B. Only Christian customs and traditions are celebrated in the UK

Q38. Christmas, Easter and New Year are religious festivals

> A. True
> B. False

Q39. Which of the following statements is true?

> A. Eid ul-fitr, Diwali and Hanukkah are Muslim, Hindu and Jewish religious festivals
> B. Eid ul-fitr, Diwali and Hanukkah are Hindu, Jewish and Muslim religious festivals

Q40. Valentine's day is when lovers exchange gifts and cards and falls on 15 February

> A. True
> B. False

Q41. Hallowe'en is on:

> A. 14 February
> B. 1 April
> C. 5 November
> D. 31 October

Q42. Guy Fawkes Night is:

> A. 14 February
> B. 5 November
> C. 11 November
> D. 31 October

Q43. Which of the following statements is true?

> A. Remembrance Day commemorates those who died fighting in the First World War.
> B. Remembrance Day commemorates those who died fighting in the First and second world wars, and other wars.

Q44. Which of the following statements is true?

> A. Remembrance Day is 11 November and is when many people wear poppies in memory of those who died from wars
> B. Remembrance Day is 5 November and is when many people wear roses in memory of those who died from wars

Q45. Which of the following statements is true?

> A. There is a United Kingdom team for Rugby, but not football
> B. There is no United Kingdom team for Rugby and football

Q46. The following four sports are very popular in the UK:

      A. Basketball, soccer, cricket and tennis
      B. Football, American Football, tennis and rugby
      C. Rugby, cricket, tennis and football
      D. Basketball, baseball, football and tennis

Q47. Most of the UK population live in the countryside

      A. True
      B. False

Q48. The population of the UK has grown by 8.5% since 1971

      A. True
      B. False

Q49. Which **two** names refer to the official church in England?

      A. Church of England
      B. Church in England
      C. Episcopal Church
      D. Anglican Church

Q50. The spiritual head of the Church of England is the:

      A. Prime Minister
      B. King or Queen
      C. The Archbishop of Canterbury
      D. Chancellor of the Exchequer

HOW THE UNITED KINGDOM IS GOVERNED

Q1. What kind of democracy best describes democracy in the UK?

      A. Westminster democracy
      B. Social democracy
      C. Multi-party democracy
      D. Parliamentary democracy

Q2. Which of the following statements is correct?

      A. The UK has a constitutional monarchy
      B. The UK has an absolute monarchy

Q3. The Head of State of the United Kingdom is the Prime Minister

      A. True
      B. False

Q4. Who appoints the government which people have chosen in democratic elections?

    A. The Prime Minister
    B. The King or Queen
    C. The Lord Chancellor
    D. The Lord High Steward

Q5. Which of the following statements is correct?

    A. The United Kingdom has had a lasting revolution, like America and France
    B. The United Kingdom has never had a lasting revolution, like America and France

Q6. Which of the following statements is correct?

    A. The British Constitution is written down in a single document
    B. The British constitution is not written down in a single document

Q7. General elections must be held at least once every:

    A. Three years
    B. Four years
    C. Five years
    D. Six years

Q8. It is optional to vote in elections in the UK

    A. True
    B. False

Q9. Which of the following statements is correct?

    A. Members of the House of Commons are part elected, part selected
    B. Members of the House of Commons are all elected

Q10. 10 Downing Street is the official home of the Queen or King

    A. True
    B. False

Q11. How many parliamentary constituencies are there in the UK?

    A. 626
    B. 636
    C. 646
    D. 656

Q12. MEPs are:

    A. Members of the House of Lords
    B. Members of the House of Commons
    C. Members of the Cabinet
    D. Members of the European Parliament

Q13. Who amongst the following is NOT a member of the cabinet?

    A. The Prime Minister
    B. The Chancellor of the Exchequer
    C. The Home Secretary
    D. The House Secretary

Q14. The second largest party in the House of Commons is called:

    A. The Opposition
    B. The Conservatives
    C. The Liberals
    D. The Opponents

Q15. The Shadow Cabinet that leads the criticism of government ministers is made up of

    A. MPs from all political parties
    B. MPs from the all parties in the House of Commons not in government
    C. MPs from the second largest party in the House of Commons
    D. MPs from the House of Lords

Q16. To stand in elections in the UK, one must be a member of a recognized political party:

    A. True
    B. False

Q17. Which of the following statements is true?

    A. Prime Minister's questions takes place every month
    B. Prime Minister's questions takes place every week

Q18. Debates in the House of Commons are chaired by the:

    A. Prime Minister
    B. The Leader of the Opposition
    C. The Lord Chancellor
    D. The Speaker

Q19. Which of the following statements is true?

    A. The Whips are MPs appointed by their party leaders to form the Cabinet or Shadow Cabinet and meet weekly to make important decisions about government policy.
    B. The Whips are MPs appointed by their party leaders and are responsible for discipline in their party and making sure MPs attend the House of Commons to vote.

Q20. The House of Lords is usually the less important of the two chambers in parliament

    A. True
    B. False

Q21. The Civil Service refers to:

    A.　Members of the British Armed forces
    B.　Managers and administrators who carry out government policy
    C.　Members of the Scottish Parliament
    D.　Assembly members of the Welsh Assembly Government

Q22. 'First past the post' refers to:

    A.　Proportional representation that ensures each party gets a number of seats in parliament proportional to number of votes received
    B.　A system were the candidate that gets the most votes in a constituency is elected an MP
    C.　By-elections arranged upon the resignation or death of a member of parliament
    D.　The appointment of Life Peers to the House of the Lords by the Prime Minister for their lifetime.

Q23. The Minister responsible for the economy is the:

    A.　Prime Minister
    B.　Chancellor of the Exchequer
    C.　The Home Secretary
    D.　The foreign Secretary

Q24. Which TWO of the following are **not** members of the Cabinet?

    A.　The Cabinet Secretary
    B.　The Education Secretary
    C.　The Permanent Secretary
    D.　The Defence Secretary

Q25. Which of the following statements is true?

    A.　There is only one parliament in the United Kingdom
    B.　There are two parliaments in the United Kingdom

Q26. Which TWO of the following countries have an Assembly?

    A.　Scotland
    B.　Wales
    C.　Northern Ireland
    D.　England

Q27. Which TWO of the following remain under central UK government control?

    A.　Health Services
    B.　Taxation
    C.　Education
    D.　Defence

Q28. Which of the following parties is not considered a major political party?

    A. The Liberal Democrats
    B. The British National Party
    C. The Labour Party
    D. The conservative party

Q29. Which of the following statements is true?

    A. The Welsh Assembly, Scottish Parliament and Northern Irish Assembly have 60 members, 129 members and 108 members respectively.
    B. The Welsh Assembly, Scottish Parliament and Northern Irish Assembly have 108 members, 60 members and 129 members respectively.

Q30. Forms of proportional representation are used to elect members to the Scottish Parliament and Welsh Assembly and this is the same method used for members of the House of Commons

    A. True
    B. False

Q31. Local government in the UK are required to provide 'mandatory' services. Which TWO of the following services are NOT mandatory services for local authorities?

    A. Social Services
    B. Defence
    C. Libraries
    D. Social Security

Q32. Local councillors are elected:

    A. Every year in June
    B. Every two years in May
    C. Every two years in June
    D. Every year in May

Q33. Which of the following domestic properties does council tax not apply?

    A. Maisonettes
    B. Houseboats
    C. Car
    D. Mobile Homes

Q34. Who decides whether someone is guilty or innocent of serious crimes?

    A. The Lord Chancellor
    B. The Judiciary
    C. A Judge
    D. A Jury

Q35. Who decides the penalty for someone found guilty of serious crimes?

    A. The Lord Chancellor
    B. The Judiciary
    C. A Judge
    D. A Jury

Q36. A judge who believes that an Act of Parliament is incompatible with the Human Rights Act can change the law

    A. True
    B. False

Q37. The judiciary is made up of judges who interpret laws made by the UK parliament

    A. True
    B. False

Q38. Which of the following statements is true?

    A. The police in the UK is organised locally and cannot be instructed by the government on what to do
    B. The police in the UK is centrally organised and is under the control of the central government

Q39. What is a quango?

    A. A government body
    B. A cabinet sub-committee
    C. A Non-departmental public body
    D. A bank of England committee

Q40. The government controls the UK press

    A. True
    B. False

Q41. At election periods, radio and television coverage is decided by:

    A. The government of the day
    B. Who owns the media house
    C. Law and is must be balanced between parties
    D. By how much parties are prepared to pay

Q42. Which of the following statements is true?

    A. Broadcasters are free to interviews politicians in a tough manner
    B. Broadcasters are not free to interviews politicians in a tough manner

Q43. Which of the following statements is true?

    A. You must be 18 to vote and majority of UK-born and naturalized citizens have full civic rights to vote
    B. You must be 17 to vote, and only UK-born citizens have full civic right to vote.

Q44. Which of the following statements is true?

    A. European Union nationals can vote in all types of election
    B. European Union nationals are not allowed to vote in general elections

Q45. In order to vote in elections, you must be registered in:

    A. The electoral book
    B. The electoral file
    C. The electoral list
    D. The electoral register

Q46. Anybody living in the UK can stand for elections

    A. True
    B. False

Q47 Elected members of parliament have a primary duty to serve their political parties

    A. True
    B. False

Q48. Which **TWO** methods below would enable you to be able to visit parliament?

    A. Writing to your local MP
    B. Turning up on the day
    C. Paying an entry fee
    D. Getting tickets from a member

Q49. The head of the commonwealth is:

    A. The Prime Minister of the United Kingdom
    B. The King or Queen
    C. The Australian Prime Minister
    D. The Canadian Prime Minister

Q50. The Commonwealth currently has:

    A. 53 member states
    B. 45 member states
    C. 50 member states
    D. 35 member states

Q51. The European Union currently has:

    A. 25 member countries
    B. 26 member countries
    C. 27 member countries
    D. 28 member countries

Q52. Which **TWO** of the following are not institutions of Europe?

    A. The European Union
    B. The European Flag
    C. The Euro
    D. The Council of Europe

Q52. Which of the following is not an institution of the European Union?

    A. The European Commission
    B. The European Parliament
    C. The Council of Europe
    D. The Council of the European Union

Q53. There are no restrictions on the right to work in any part of the European Union to Citizens of and EU member state.

    A. True
    B. False

Q53. European Union law is legally binding in the UK and all other member states

    A. True
    B. False

Q54. Elections to the European Parliament takes place every:

    A. 2 years
    B. 3 years
    C. 4 years
    D. 5 years

Q55. The Civil Service of the European Union is called:

    A. The European Parliament
    B. The Council of Europe
    C. The Council of the European Union
    D. The European Commission

Q56. The European Convention on Human Rights was drawn up by the:

    A. The European Parliament
    B. The Council of Europe
    C. The Council of the European Union
    D. The European Commission

Q57. Which of the following statements is true?

    A. All member states of the Council of Europe are bound by the European Convention of Human rights
    B. All member states of the Council of Europe can opt out of being bound by the European Convention of Human rights

Q58. The United Nations is an international organisation of about:

    A. 175 member countries
    B. 180 member countries
    C. 185 member countries
    D. 190 member countries

Q59. The UK is a permanent member of the UN Security Council

    A. True
    B. False

Q60. Which of the following is not an agreement of the United Nations?

    A. Convention on Human Rights
    B. Universal Declaration of Human Rights
    C. Convention on the Elimination of All Forms of Discrimination against Women
    D. Convention on the Rights of the Child

EVERYDAY NEEDS

Q1. The proportion of people who own their home in the UK is closest to:

    A. 1 in 2
    B. 2 in 3
    C. 1 in 4
    D. 2 in 5

Q2. How do people usually buy their homes in the UK?

    A. Using Cash that has been saved up themselves
    B. Using a Loan provided by the government
    C. Using a Mortgage, which is a special bank loan
    D. Using a loan provided by the seller of the home

Q3. Estate agents represent the buyers of homes

    A. True
    B. False

Q4. Who should you contact first if you want to buy a home in Scotland?

    A. An Estate Agent
    B. The Seller of the house
    C. A solicitor
    D. The local authority

Q5. Which of the following statements is correct?

    A. In the UK, you always make an offer lower than what the seller of a home is asking
    B. You can make an offer higher than what the seller is asking

Q6. Which of the following statements is correct?

    A. You can withdraw an offer on a home anytime everywhere in the UK
    B. In some regions of the UK, an offer becomes legally binding earlier than others

Q7. Which TWO of the following should you employ to purchase a home?

    A. An accountant
    B. A solicitor
    C. A bank Manager
    D. A surveyor

Q8. A landlord is some who owns land in the UK

    A. True
    B. False

Q9. Which of the following statements is correct?

    A. You can rent property from the local authority, housing association or private property owners
    B. You can only rent property from private property owners

Q10. Everyone is entitled to apply for council housing

    A. True
    B. False

Q11. Share ownership schemes are run by:

    A. The central government
    B. The local authority
    C. Private property owners
    D. Housing associations

Q12. Which TWO are names for a document signed when renting private accommodation?

    A. Renting agreement
    B. Lease
    C. Tenancy agreement
    D. Contract agreement

Q13. How much deposit should you expect to pay to the Landlord at the beginning of a tenancy if you are renting private accommodation?

    A. Half a month's rent
    B. One month's rent
    C. One and a half month's rent
    D. Two month's rent

Q14. It is a criminal offence for a landlord to use threats to force a tenant to leave without a court order

    A. True
    B. False

Q15. A landlord is allowed to discriminate against a potential tenant based on his religion

    A. True
    B. False

Q16. If you are homeless, which organisation has legal a duty to offer help and advice?

    A. Housing Associations
    B. Citizens Advice Bureau
    C. Local authority
    D. Shelter

Q17. You can pay for water supply to your home by instalments or by a lump sump

    A. True
    B. False

Q18. Which of the following services is provided by the local authority?

    A. Water
    B. Gas
    C. Electricity
    D. Refuse collection

Q19. Which of the following statements is true?

    A. The only funding available to local government for service provision is from council tax
    B. Local government services are paid for partly by Council Tax and central government grants

Q20. Waste recycling involves you separating your rubbish and placing it at the back of your house for collection

        A. True
        B. False

Q21.The amount of Council Tax paid on a house depends on:

        A. The location of the property
        B. The number of people staying at the property
        C. The size and value of the property
        D. The amount of income earned by the breadwinner

Q22. Which TWO of the following people can claim a reduction on the Council Tax they pay?

        A. A disabled person
        B. Someone on a low income
        C. A single person staying at a property
        D. Tenants

Q23. When a property is bought with a mortgage, it is compulsory to:

        A. Insure the contents of the home
        B. Insure the building
        C. Insure both the buildings and the contents of the home
        D. Insure neither the building or its contents

Q24. If you have problems with your neighbours, you should first speak to the:

        A. Police if you own the home
        B. Landlord if renting
        C. Housing association or local authority
        D. Neighbours for an amicable solution

Q25. Which of the following statements is true?

        A. Information on how to pay bills is only available by contacting the company that has sent the bill
        B. Information on how to pay bills is normally found on the back of the bill

Q26. Which TWO of the following are standard bank notes in the UK?

        A. £1
        B. £5
        C. £50
        D. £2

Q27. Which TWO of the following countries use the Euro?

    A. England
    B. Scotland
    C. Republic of Ireland
    D. France

Q28. Bank Notes in issued in Scotland are valid everywhere in the UK, but those issued in Northern Ireland are not.

    A. True
    B. False

Q29. Which of the following statements is true?

    A. Debit cards, credit cards and store cards represent different names for the same thing
    B. Debit cards, credit cards and store cards are different ways of paying for things.

Q30. To open a bank account, you only need to show your passport, driving licence or immigration document to prove your identity.

    A. True
    B. False

Q31. Which TWO of the following are similar in the way they are used, except that one is used in a specific shop?

    A. Cash Card
    B. Credit Card
    C. Debit Card
    D. Store Card

Q32. Which of the following organisations does not normally make loans out to people in the UK?

    A. Banks
    B. Building Societies
    C. Credit Unions
    D. Insurance companies

Q33. A credit union is controlled by their:

    A. Partners
    B. Members
    C. Shareholders
    D. Creditors

Q34. For which of the following is insurance compulsory in the UK?

  A. Building insurance
  B. Car insurance
  C. Contents insurance
  D. Travel insurance

Q35. Social security is best described as:

  A. A social system where people in a neighbourhood form an association
  B. A system of fairness where the rich are taxed to pay the poor
  C. A government program that provides benefits to retirees and the disabled
  D. A system which pays benefits to people who do not have enough to live on

Q36. Who amongst the following people would typically not be able to access welfare benefits?

  A. Sick and disabled people
  B. Older people
  C. Low income workers
  D. Foreign student

Q37. Which TWO places can you go to if you need a guide to benefits?

  A. Bank
  B. Jobcentre Plus offices
  C. Post Office
  D. Citizens Bureau

Q38. Which of the following statements is true?

  A. The National Health Service (NHS) started in 1949 and provides free healthcare to everyone
  B. The National Health Service (NHS) started in 1948 and provides free healthcare to residents

Q39. Another name for the family doctor normally used in the UK is:

  A. A General Doctor (GD)
  B. A General Pharmacist (GP)
  C. A General Practitioner (GP)
  D. A General Physician (GP)

Q40. If you need advice on health matters, which of the following options would not be ideal initially?

  A. Ask your local pharmacist
  B. Speak to an NHS nurse via NHS direct
  C. Seek advice from the Citizens Advice Bureau
  D. Use NHS Direct Online

Q41. In order to see a specialist in a hospital, you must first see your:

    A. Pharmacist
    B. Nurse
    C. Chemist
    D. GP

Q42. Which of the following statements is true?

    A. You should register with a GP as soon as possible after you move to a new area.
    B. Registration is not necessary, and can wait until you require treatment.

Q43. Which of the following statements is true?

    A. Free prescriptions are available to everyone in the UK
    B. Free prescriptions are only available to a select group of people

Q44. Which of the following statements is true?

    A. You should not go directly to the hospital under any circumstances, even in an emergency but should call an ambulance (999).
    B. You may go directly to a hospital's Accident and Emergency (A&E) in an emergency without a GP's letter

Q45. Your pharmacist has advised you that you need to pay for your medicine. This is most likely because:

    A. You are 22 years old and live in Wales
    B. You are a working 18 year old and live in England
    C. Aged 60 years and 2 months
    D. Had a baby 11 months ago

Q46. NHS direct can be accessed via the Internet and NHS direct online over the telephone

    A. True
    B. False

Q47 Which **TWO** numbers could you dial in the case of an emergency?

    A. 199
    B. 911
    C. 999
    D. 112

Q48. Which method is not suggested as a way of finding a dentists or optician?

    A. Asking at the local library
    B. Asking at the Citizens advice bureau
    C. Using NHS direct
    D. Using the Yellow Pages

Q49. Most people have to pay for sight tests and glasses with some exceptions

> A. True
> B. False

Q50. Who may be required to pay for dental treatment?

> A. Someone receiving child benefit
> B. Mother of 9 month old baby
> C. Someone on income support
> D. Someone who is 22 and lives in Wales

Q51. Ante-natal care refers to services for pregnant women

> A. True
> B. False

Q52. Antenatal care is NOT typically available from which of the following places

> A. Local hospital
> B. Special clinics
> C. Local health centre
> D. Pharmacy

Q53. All GPs in the UK are required to provide antenatal care

> A. True
> B. False

Q54. Who amongst the following people may not provide much support for a pregnant woman?

> A. Midwife
> B. Chemist
> C. GP
> D. Health visitor

Q55. Information on pregnancy is available from a number of organisations. Which one would you not contact about pregnancy?

> A. National Childbirth Trust
> B. Local health authority
> C. Social Security Office
> D. Local Surgery

Q56. You must register your baby with the Registrar of Births, Marriages and Deaths (Register Office) within ten weeks of the birth of a child

> A. True
> B. False

Q57. In all cases, both parents' names must be on a child's birth certificate

      A. True
      B. False

Q58. Education in the UK (except Northern Ireland) is free and compulsory for children between the ages of

      A. 4 and 18
      B. 5 and 17
      C. 5 and 16
      D. 6 and 16

Q59. Which TWO of the following may be prosecuted if a child does not go to school?

      A. The Head teacher
      B. The Child's guardian
      C. The Child's parent
      D. The Child

Q60. Which of the following statements is true?

      A. The education system in the UK is the same in all the four home countries
      B. The education system in the UK is different in all the four home countries

Q61. There are two major stages for compulsory education in The UK. They are called:

      A. First and Second
      B. Key stage 1 and Key stage 2
      C. Primary and Secondary
      D. Basic and advanced

Q62. In Northern Ireland, the compulsory age for education for all children is between 4 and 16 years

      A. True
      B. False

Q63. Which of the following statements does not accurately describe the age range for primary education in the UK?

      A. Primary stage lasts from 5 to 11 in England
      B. Primary stage lasts from 6 to 11 in Wales
      C. Primary stage lasts from 5 to 12 in Scotland
      D. Primary stage lasts from 4 to 11 in Northern Ireland

Q64. Which of the following statements is true about mixed sex schools?

      A. These are schools where the teachers are both male and female
      B. These are schools where boys and girls study together in the same classes

Q65. At what age do students leave secondary education in the UK?

    A. 14
    B. 15
    C. 16
    D. 17

Q66. Education in every school in the UK is free

    A. True
    B. False

Q67. Which TWO of the following are private fee-paying schools?

    A. State schools
    B. Independent schools
    C. Faith schools
    D. Public schools

Q68. General information about schools and education can best be obtained from:

    A. Social Security office
    B. Local education authority
    C. Department for Children, Schools and Families
    D. Citizens Bureau

Q69. Which TWO of the following do parents have to pay for in state schools?

    A. Tuition
    B. School uniforms
    C. School books
    D. Sports wear

Q70. Admission arrangements vary from area to area in the UK

    A. True
    B. False

Q71. Which of the following schools is NOT a faith school?

    A. A Christian school
    B. A Muslim school
    C. A Grammar school
    D. A Jewish school

Q72. At independent schools, parents must pay the full cost of their child's education.

    A. True
    B. False

Q73. What percentage of children in the UK go to approximately 2500 independent schools in the UK?

> A. 8%
> B. 12%
> C. 16%
> D. 20%

Q74. The National Curriculum is NOT followed in which of the following countries?

> A. England
> B. Scotland
> C. Northern Ireland
> D. Wales

Q75. All state primary and secondary schools follow the National Curriculum (in countries where it applies?

> A. True
> B. False

Q76. Schools are required by law to provide religious education for all pupils?

> A. True
> B. False

Q77. How many stages does the curriculum in England Have?

> A. Two
> B. Three
> C. Four
> D. Five

Q78. Key stage tests are done in England at which ages?

> A. 6,11,13 and 16
> B. 7,11, 14 and 16
> C. 7, 12, 15 and 17
> D. 6, 12, 14 and 17

Q79. Which of the following statements is true?

> A. In Scotland, there is a national curriculum that is prescribed by law for schools
> B. In Scotland, a broad curriculum informed by national guidance is used in schools

Q80. GCSE and A levels are done at what ages in England?

> A. 17 and 18
> B. 18 and 19
> C. 16 and 18
> D. 15 and 17

Q81. Key stage tests for 7 and 11 year olds have been abolished in which home country?

> A. England
> B. Scotland
> C. Northern Ireland
> D. Wales

Q82. A curriculum for excellence (for 3 -18 year olds) is intended to be used in which home country?

> A. England
> B. Scotland
> C. Northern Ireland
> D. Wales

Q83. What do 14 to 16 year olds currently do in Scotland to further their education?

> A. GCSEs
> B. Key stage Four
> C. A levels
> D. Standard Grade

Q84. In Scotland the first phase for children from 5 to 14 is divided into how many levels?

> A. Four
> B. Five
> C. Six
> D. Seven

Q85. For how many days in a year must schools be open?

> A. 190
> B. 195
> C. 200
> D. 205

Q86. Which of the following statements is true?

> A. The Head teacher of a schools decides how the a school is run and administered
> B. The Governing body of a school decides how the a school is run and administered

Q87. Which TWO of the following may decide term dates for schools?

> A. The Head Teacher
> B. The Department for Children, Schools and Families
> C. The local education authority
> D. The governing body

Q88. Parents have a number of places reserved for them on the governing bodies of schools in England. The equivalent of a governing body in Scotland is called:

    A. The School Council
    B. The School Authority
    C. The School Board
    D. The School Governors

Q89. Which of the following statements is true?

    A. At 16, young people decide whether to go to university or to take a gap year
    B. At 16, young people decide whether to go for A levels or leave school

Q90. Further education colleges offer a variety of courses for improving skills, including language.

    A. True
    B. False

Q91. ESOL stands for:

    A. English as a standard of languages
    B. English standard for overseas learners
    C. English as a second official language
    D. English for speakers of other languages

Q92. Which of the following statements is true?

    A. Financial assistance (Education Maintenance Allowance) is available to young people from low income families up till age 19
    B. Financial assistance (Education Maintenance Allowance) is available to young people from low income families up till age 21

Q93. Which of the following courses would typically not be available from an adult education class?

    A. Medical training
    B. Language training
    C. Numeracy training
    D. Computing training

Q94. University in the UK is started at what age?

    A. 18
    B. 19
    C. 20
    D. Any age above 18

Q95. What is maximum amount that universities can charge students for tuition (2006/2007 academic year)?

        A. No fees
        B. £1500
        C. £2000
        D. £3000

Q96. In which country is there no tuition fees for university?

        A. England
        B. Northern Ireland
        C. Scotland
        D. Wales

Q97. Which of the following statements is true?

        A. Students must pay for university tuition while attending university, even if it involves getting into debt.
        B. Students do not have to pay anything before or during studies, but after leaving university.

Q98. The government pays tuition fees for students at university and charges students after they have started working

        A. True
        B. False

Q99. Which of the following ways is NOT a usual way of paying for tuition fees while at university?

        A. Grant
        B. Bursary
        C. Low-interest student loan
        D. Government assistance

Q100. At what age do all children get career advice?

        A. 12
        B. 13
        C. 14
        D. 15

Q101. A child in the UK is allowed to watch any film at the cinema or any DVD.

        A. True
        B. False

Q102. Which of the following is NOT a classification for films?

        A. U
        B. 18R
        C. PG
        D. 12

Q103. Which of the following statements is true?

    A. A film classified as 12A may not be seen at the cinema or rented by someone under the age of 12.

    B. A film classified as 12A may be seen or rented by someone under the age of 12 if they are with an adult.

Q104. Which TWO of the following people DO NOT have to pay for a TV license?

    A. Someone watching colour television, aged 75 years

    B. Someone watching television from DVD players only

    C. Someone using a computer, occasionally to receive TV broadcasts

    D. Someone using a mobile phone, occasionally to receive TV broadcasts

Q105. A television licence needs to be renewed every:

    A.   3 months

    B. 4 months

    C. 6 months

    D. 12 months

Q106. Which of the following statements is true?

    A. Blind people can receive a 50% discount on their TV licence

    B. Blind people can receive a 100% discount on their TV licence

Q107. Which of the following statements is true?

    A. Watching TV without a licence is a criminal offence

    B. Watching TV without a licence is a civil offence

Q108. The National Trust is a charity that:

    A. Maintains museums and some tourist attractions in the UK

    B. Works to preserve important buildings and countryside in the UK

    C. Works to provide information on sports, clubs and societies in the UK

    D. Provides national lottery services from which large prizes can be won.

Q109. People under what age are not allowed to buy alcohol in a supermarket?

    A. 16

    B. 17

    C. 18

    D. 21

Q110. Someone aged 16 can drink wine or beer with a meal in a hotel or restaurant.

    A. True

    B. False

Q111. People under what age are not allowed into betting shops or gambling clubs?

        A. 16
        B. 17
        C. 18
        D. 21

Q112. What is the minimum age for buying a national lottery ticket?

        A. 16
        B. 17
        C. 18
        D. 21

Q113. Many people in the UK have pets such as cats and dogs

        A. True
        B. False

Q114. Which TWO groups do veterinary surgeons (vets) provide vaccination and medical treatments for?

        A. Cats
        B. Students
        C. Mothers
        D. Dogs

Q115. Which of the following statements is true?

        A. It is against British law to treat pets cruelly
        B. There are no laws relating to the treatment of pets

Q116. Information about trains can be obtained from which organisation?

        A. National transport union
        B. British rail
        C. National trains
        D. National rail

Q117. Which of the following groups of people is NOT likely to qualify for discounted train tickets?

        A. Students
        B. Pensioners
        C. Families
        D. Secretaries

Q118. Which of the following statements is true?

        A. All taxes and minicabs must be licensed to operate lawfully
        B. Only black cabs need to be licensed to operate lawfully

Q119. What is the minimum age for driving a lorry or bus?

        A. 17
        B. 18
        C. 20
        D. 21

Q120. What is the minimum age for driving a car or motorcycle?

        A. 17
        B. 18
        C. 20
        D. 21

Q121. What is the minimum age for driving a medium-sized lorry?

        A. 17
        B. 18
        C. 20
        D. 21

Q122. You must have a driving licence to drive on public roads

        A. True
        B. False

Q123. Which of the following statements is true?

        A. You are required to pass only a practical test in order to get a full driving licence.
        B. You are required to pass a theory and practical test in order to get a full driving licence.

Q124. The correct order for obtaining a full driving licence in the UK would be:

        A. Pass theory test, pass practical test, the apply for provisional licence
        B. Apply for provisional licence, pass practical test, then pass theory test
        C. Pass theory test, apply for provisional licence, then pass practical test
        D. Apply for provisional licence, pass theory test, then pass practical test

Q125. Which of the following statements is true?

        A. Once you get a licence, it can be used until the age of 75 upon which it is renewed every three years.
        B. Once you get a licence, it can be used until the age of 70 upon which it is renewed every three years.

Q126. If you hold an overseas licence from a non-European Union country, you are allowed to drive with it for a maximum of

A. 6 months
B. 12 months
C. 24 months
D. 36 months

Q127. Holders of driving licences from a country in the EU can drive without getting a UK driving licence for as long as their licence is valid.

A. True
B. False

Q128. Which of the following statements is true?

A. It is a criminal offence to drive a car without proper motor insurance
B. Motor insurance is optional like other types of insurance in the UK

Q129. A Ministry of Transport (MOT) test is required annually form approved garages for vehicles older than:

A. 3 years old
B. 5 years old
C. 6 years old
D. 10 years old

Q130. Where could you go to pay for road tax?

A. The bank
B. The post office
C. Some approved retail shops
D. An approved garage

Q131. Which of the following statements is true?

A. An MOT certificate is optional and does not affect your auto insurance.
B. An MOT certificate is compulsory, and not having one is an offence and
invalidates your auto insurance.

Q132. Which of the following statements is true about seat belts?

A. Only those in the front seat of a vehicle need to wear seat belts
B. Everyone in a vehicle should wear seat belts

Q133. Motorcyclists and their passengers are required by law to wear crash helmets. Who does this law not apply to?

    A. Experienced cyclists with 10 years experience
    B. Women who have long hair
    C. Motorcyclists making distances shorter than 10 miles
    D. Sikh men wearing a turban

Q134. It is illegal to drive while holding a mobile phone in the UK

    A. True
    B. False

Q135. Drivers are allowed to use their judgement to decide what speeds to drive at on UK roads

    A. True
    B. False

Q136. Being 'over the limit' refers to:

    A. Driving too fast above the speed limit
    B. Smoking heavily while driving
    C. An MOT test that fails due to excessive exhaust fumes
    D. A driver having more than the permitted amount of alcohol

Q137. The police stop a man to check his alcohol limit while driving. A name for such a test is:

    A. An intoxicates test
    B. A Drinking test
    C. A Blood test
    D. A breathalyser test

Q138. Which of these speed limits for cars and motorcycles is correct (in miles per hour)?

    A. 30 mph in built-up areas, 50 mph on single carriageways and 60 mph on motorways
    B. 30 mph in built-up areas, 60 mph on single carriageways and 70 mph on motorways
    C. 40 mph in built-up areas, 60 mph on single carriageways and 70 mph on motorways
    D. 40 mph in built-up areas, 70 mph on single carriageways and 80 mph on motorways

Q139. The speed limit for buses, Lorries and cars pulling caravans is lower than standard speed limits

    A. True
    B. False

Q140. Which TWO numbers can you call in the event of an injury to contact the ambulance services or police?

    A. 199
    B. 911
    C. 112
    D. 999

Q141. It is a criminal offence to be involved in an accident and not stop while driving

    A. True
    B. False

Q142 If involved in an accident, it is better to admit fault to the other driver

    A. True
    B. False

Q143. Which of the following statements is true?

    A. If involved in an accident, exchange names, addresses, vehicle registration numbers and insurance details with the other driver
    B. If involved in an accident, do not exchange names, addresses, vehicle registration numbers and insurance details with the other driver

Q144. It is compulsory for every UK citizen to carry an identity card

    A. True
    B. False

Q145. Which TWO of the following documents can be used to prove one's identity?

    A. A credit card
    B. A National Insurance number card
    C. A provisional driving licence
    D. A bank statement

EMPLOYMENT

Q1. Anyone is entitled to work in the UK:

    A. True
    B. False

Q2. Which of the following places would you not likely find job advertisements?

    A. Local and national newspapers
    B. Local Jobcentre Plus
    C. Local Bank
    D. Employment agencies

Q3. NARIC stands for

    A. National Academic Recognition Information Centre
    B. National Academic Review Information Centre
    C. National Rehabilitation Information Centre
    D. National Academic Recognition Information Company

Q4. Which organisation should you contact if you have a qualification from overseas and would like to know how they compare with UK qualifications?

    A. An Employment Agency
    B. Jobcentre Plus
    C. NARIC
    D. Department for Work and Pensions

Q5. Which organisation should you contact if you need advice in finding and applying for jobs as well as claiming benefits?

    A. An Employment Agency
    B. Jobcentre Plus
    C. NARIC
    D. Department for Children, Schools and Families

Q6. A curriculum vitae (CV) is a document that gives details of your education, qualifications and previous employment, skills and interest

    A. True
    B. False

Q7. Which of the following statements is correct?

    A. A referee for a job application can be anyone who knows you well and is happy to write a reference
    B. A referee for a job application should be someone who is not a family member or personal friend

Q8. It is normal to exaggerate your experience at a job interview and once you have the job, there are no further consequences

    A. True
    B. False

Q9. Which of the following statements is correct?

  A. A criminal record check is also called a Criminal Records Bureau check
  B. A criminal record check is also called a Criminal Records Background check

Q10. Which organisation would you NOT contact primarily for training opportunities?

  A. Your local library
  B. Your local college
  C. Learn direct
  D. Department for Work and Pensions

Q11. Volunteering can be a positive influence when applying for paid jobs in the future

  A. True
  B. False

Q12. Women can be paid less than men who do the same job on the basis of gender only

  A. True
  B. False

Q13. In which of the following cases would discrimination laws not apply?

  A. Working in a supermarket
  B. Working in a law firm
  C. Working in someone's home
  D. Working in a school

 Q14. It is against the law for an employer to discriminate against someone on the basis of sex, disability, religion, sexual orientation and age

  A. True
  B. False

Q15. Which of the following pairs of commissions and discrimination is not correct?

  A. The commission for Racial Equality and racial discrimination
  B. The Equal opportunities commission and age discrimination
  C. The Disability Right commission and disability discrimination
  D. The Equal opportunities commission and sex discrimination

Q16. From October 2007, one commission would address discrimination. What is it called?

  A. The Equality Commission
  B. Equal Opportunities Commission
  C. Commission for Equality and Human Rights
  D. The Commission against Discrimination

Q17. In Northern Ireland, one commission provides information and advice on all forms of unlawful discrimination. It is called the:

    A. The Equality Commission
    B. Equal Opportunities Commission
    C. Commission for Equality and Human Rights
    D. The Commission against unlawful Discrimination

Q18. Only women can experience sexual harassment in the workplace

    A. True
    B. False

Q19. Which of the following statements is true?

    A. Employers are responsible for the behaviour of their employees while they are at work
    B. Employees are responsible for their individual behaviour while they are at work

Q20. Which TWO of the following organisations could you contact for advice and support related to sexual discrimination?

    A. Jobcentre Plus
    B. Citizens Advice Bureau
    C. Equal Opportunities Commission
    D. Department for Work and Pensions

Q21. Which of the following may not qualify as a form of sexual harassment?

    A. Comments about your looks that are uncomfortable
    B. Comments or question s about your sexual orientation
    C. Comments about your performance at work
    D. Comments that are rude or hostile because of your gender

Q22. Which of the following statements is true?

    A. Employers and employees both have legal responsibilities at work
    B. Only employees have legal responsibilities at work

Q23   Within how many months of starting a new job should your employer give you a written contract or statement?

    A. One months
    B. Two months
    C. Three months
    D. Four months

Q24. Which of the following statements is true?

    A. The contract or written statement is useful in solving disputes between employer and employee.
    B. The contract or written statement is purely for informational purposes and may not be relevant in a dispute.

Q25. What is the minimum wage per hour for workers aged 22 and above (October 2006)?

        A. £5.05
        B. £5.15
        C. £5.25
        D. £5.35

Q26. What is the minimum wage per hour for workers aged 18-21 (October 2006)?

        A. £4.35
        B. £4.45
        C. £4.55
        D. £4.65

Q27. What is the minimum wage per hour for workers aged 16-17 (October 2006)?

        A. £3.00
        B. £3.10
        C. £3.20
        D. £3.30

Q28. Which of the following statements is true?

        A. You are obliged to work more hours than the hours agreed on your contract
        B. It is up to an employee to agree to work more hours than agreed on a contract.

Q29. Which TWO pieces of information is required to be displayed on a payslip

        A. Tax payment
        B. Job description
        C. Holiday entitlement
        D. National Insurance payments

Q30. It is illegal to pay your employees less than the national minimum wage

        A. True
        B. False

Q31. Employees who are 16 or older are entitled to how at least how many weeks paid holiday?

        A. Two weeks
        B. Three weeks
        C. Four weeks
        D. Five weeks

Q32. The government department responsible for collection of taxes is called:

    A. HM Secret Service
    B. Department for Work and Pensions
    C. Border and Immigration Agency
    D. HM Revenue and Customs

Q33. For most people, tax is automatically deducted from earnings by the employer and paid to the government

    A. True
    B. False

Q34. Government collects tax in order to raise money for government services such as roads, education, police and armed forces.

    A. True
    B. False

Q35. National Insurance contributions are used to pay for which of the following services?

    A. State Retirement Pensions
    B. Education
    C. Police
    D. Armed Forces

Q36. Which of the following Benefits would not be affected by how much National Insurance contributions paid?

    A. State Retirement Pensions
    B. Child Benefit
    C. Jobseeker's Allowance
    D. Maternity Pay

Q37. Which TWO places is it possible to get a National Insurance number from?

    A. Local Social Security Office
    B. Jobcentre Plus
    C. Local Education Authority office
    D. Citizens Advice Bureau

Q38. National Insurance contributions are compulsory for almost everyone in paid work in the UK

    A. True
    B. False

Q39. Which of the following statements is true?

    A. State Pension age for men and women is currently 65 years
    B. State Pension age for men is 65 and for women is currently 60 years

Q40. By 2020, the State Pension age for men and women would be:

    A. 65 years
    B. 67 years
    C. 70 years
    D. 75 years

Q41. Where is it best to get information about State Pensions?

    A. HM Revenue and Customs
    B. Department for Children, Schools and Families
    C. The Pension Service
    D. Citizens Advice Bureau

Q42. Which of the following statements is true?

    A. In addition to a State Pensions, occupational pension schemes and personal pension schemes also exist
    B. The only pension available to a pensioner is the State Pension

Q43. The Pension Advisory Service is another name for the Pension Service

    A. True
    B. False

Q44. Which of the following people may not be the best to talk to regarding issues related to health and safety at the workplace or other problems at work?

    A. Your bank manager
    B. Your supervisor
    C. Your manager
    D. A trade union representative

Q45. Which of the following statements is true?

    A. A trade union is an organisation that aims to influence the government in order to pass regulation favourable for an industrial sector.
    B. A trade union is an organisation that aims to improve the pay and working conditions of their members.

Q46. Where can you find details of trade unions if you want to join one?

    A. Trades Union Council
    B. Trades Union Company
    C. Trades Union Cooperative
    D. Trades Union Congress

Q47. Which organisation is best able to give you information about your rights at work?

      A. Citizens Advice Bureau (CAB)
      B. The national Advisory, Conciliation and Arbitration Service (ACAS)
      C. Department for Work and Pensions (DWP)
      D. Trades Union Congress (TUC)

Q48. Which of the following statements is true?

      A. An employee can be dismissed immediately for serious misconduct at work
      B. An employee must be issued a warning letter first before dismissal for any reason

Q49. It is illegal for an employee to dismiss an employee without good cause

      A. True
      B. False

Q50. Which of the following would not be a good reason for an employer to dismiss an employee?

      A. Persistent lateness to work
      B. Inability to do the job properly
      C. Requesting a pay increase
      D. Pilfering employer resources

Q51. If you feel you have been unfairly dismissed at work, how long do you normally have to complain?

      A. 3 months
      B. 6 months
      C. 9 months
      D. 12 months

Q52. Which allowance can most people who become unemployed and are actively seeking work get?

      A. Child Benefit
      B. Jobseekers allowance
      C. Income support
      D. Jobseekers pay

Q53. Which organisation specializes in employment matters and may award you compensation for unfair dismissal?

      A. County court
      B. Employment court
      C. The national Advisory, Conciliation and Arbitration Service (ACAS)
      D. Employment Tribunal

Q54. Which TWO of the following reasons for losing a job would be classified as redundancy?

        A. Job loss resulting from poor job performance
        B. Job loss resulting from the closure of a business unit
        C. Job loss resulting from the company unable to afford payments
        D. Job loss resulting from serious misconduct

Q55. Which of the following statements is true?

        A. The amount of redundancy pay received is dependent on length of time of employment
        B. The amount of redundancy pay received is a flat rate independent of length of time of employment

Q56. Which of the following statements is true?

        A. Self-employed people are responsible for paying their own tax and National Insurance
        B. Self-employed people do not have to pay tax and National Insurance

Q57. Who is best able to assist a self-employed person in his tax matters?

        A. An independent financial adviser
        B. A Banker
        C. A business consultant
        D. An accountant

Q58. Which TWO organisations would be most appropriate for advice and support on setting up, funding and running a business?

        A. A bank
        B. Business Link
        C. Your local library
        D. HM Revenue and Customs

Q59. Self-employed people are responsible for keeping detailed records of earnings and spending and send their business accounts to HM revenue and customs every two years.

        A. True
        B. False

Q60. British citizens need a work permit to work in other countries that are members of the European Economic Area (EEA)

        A. True
        B. False

Q61. Only mothers have a right to time off work after their children are born?

        A. True
        B. False

Q62. How long is the maternity leave that women are entitled to when expecting a baby for antenatal care?

        A. 24 weeks
        B. 25 weeks
        C. 26 weeks
        D. 27 weeks

Q63. Which of the following statements is true?

        A. Fathers are entitled to two weeks **paid** paternity leave when their child is born, provided they have worked for a company for 26 weeks
        B. Fathers are entitled to two weeks **unpaid** paternity leave when their child is born, provided they have worked for a company for 26 weeks

Q64. Which of the following statements is true?

        A. Maternity leave is only available to full time working women
        B. Maternity leave is available to both part-time and full time working women

Q65. Which of the following statements is true?

        A. All women on maternity leave are paid for the period they are on leave
        B. Some women on maternity leave are paid for the period they are on leave

Q66. The minimum age for children to do paid work is

        A. 13 years
        B. 14 years
        C. 15 years
        D. 16 years

Q67. Which TWO of the following jobs are 14-16 year children allowed to do?

        A. Selling alcohol
        B. Newspaper delivery
        C. Working in a supermarket
        D. Working in a kitchen

Q68. There are strict laws to protect children from exploitation and ensure that work does not affect their education

        A. True
        B. False

Q69. Which of the following statements would not apply to working children (14-16 year olds) within the legal framework?

    A. They must not work before 8a.m. or after 8p.m.
    B. They must not work for more than one hour before school starts
    C. They must not work for more than 12 hours in any school week
    D. They must not work for more than 2 hours on any school day or a Sunday

Q70. Which of the following statements is true?

    A. Children aged 14-16 years should not work for more than 4 hours without a one-hour rest break
    B. Children aged 14-16 years should not work for more than 5 hours without a one-hour rest break

Q71. Which of the following statements is true?

    A. Children who work only need an employment card from their local authority
    B. Children who work need both an employment card from their local authority and a medical certificate of fitness for work

Q72. Who has a duty to ensure that the law is being obeyed with regards to working children?

    A. Department for Work and Pensions
    B. The Local Authority
    C. HM Revenue and Customs
    D. Border and Immigration Agency

Q73. It is government policy to help people with childcare responsibilities to take up work

    A. True
    B. False

Q74. New Deal is a government programme that aims to help which group of people?

    A. The Self-employed
    B. Pensioners
    C. New mothers and fathers
    D. The unemployed

Q75. Which of the following statements is true?

    A. Children under 14 are not allowed to work under any circumstances
    B. Children under 14 may be allowed to do some work provided a licence is received from the local authority

Chapter 3 Answers with book* paragraph reference

*LIFE IN THE UNITED KINGDOM – A journey to Citizenship Second edition ISBN-978-0-11-341313-3

A CHANGING SOCIETY

Q1. D - Before 1945 Page 27, paragraph 2

Q2. C- 51% Page 29, paragraph 4

Q3. B – False Page 29, paragraph 4

Q4. B – India Page 28, paragraph 1 and 2

Q5. C - United States, Australia, South Africa and New Zealand Page 28, paragraph 3

Q6. A – True Page 28, paragraph 3

Q7. B – 1857 Page 29, paragraph 1

Q8. C – 1882 Page 29, paragraph 1

Q9. B – False Page 29, paragraph 2. 'Suffragettes' are women who campaigned for greater rights, especially the right to vote

Q10. D – 1918 Page 29, paragraph 2

Q11. C – 1928 Page 29, paragraph 2

Q12. B – False Page 29, paragraph 2. Voting age was 21 at that time

Q13. B – False Page 29, paragraph 3

Q14. C – 45% Page 29, paragraph 4

Q15. A – True Page 29, paragraph 5

Q16. D -20% Page 29, paragraph 6

Q17. A – True Page 29, paragraph 6

Q18. C – 15 million Page 30, paragraph 1

Q19. D – 25% Page 29, paragraph 2

Q20. B – False Page 30, paragraph 3

Q21. C – 5 and 16 Page 30, paragraph 5

Q22. A – True Page 30, paragraph 2

Q23. B – False Page 30, paragraph 4

Q24. C – 75% Page 29, paragraph 5

Q25. A – True Page 29, paragraph 6

Q26. B – 7, 11 and 14 Page 30, paragraph 5

Q27. B – False Page 30, paragraph 5. Teachers asses children at ages 7 and 11 and national tests at age 14

Q28. D – 1 in 3 Page 31, paragraph 4

Q29. B – 17 and 18 Page 31, paragraph 1

Q30. D – General Certificate of Education at an Advanced level Page 31, paragraph 1

Q31. B – False Page 31, paragraph 6

Q32. C – Work in supermarkets and newsagents Page 31, paragraph 6

Q33. A – True Page 31, paragraph 7

Q34. B – False Page 31, paragraph 10. Smoking in some places is not allowed

Q35. C – Smoking has decreased for adults, but has increased for young people Page 31, paragraph 10

Q36. B – Girls Page 31, paragraph 10

Q37. B – 16 years old Page 31, paragraph 10

Q38. D – 18 years old Page 32, paragraph 1

Q39. A – 10% Page 30, paragraph 2

Q40. C – Drinking a lot of alcohol at a time Page 32, paragraph 1

Q41. C – Deferring university entrance by a year Page 31, paragraph 4

Q42. A –Heroin and C – Cannabis Page 32, paragraph 2. Some other illegal drugs are cocaine, ecstasy and amphetamines

Q43. A – True Page 32, paragraph 3

Q44. C – 50% Page 32, paragraph 2. A third of all the population is estimated to have used illegal drugs at some point in time

Q45. A –Drugs misuse is a serious issue for British society Page 32, paragraph 3

Q46. C – 18 Page 33, paragraph 1

Q47. D – 1 in 5 Page 33, paragraph 1

Q48. A – Young people have little interest in party politics Page 33, paragraph 2

Q49. A – Immigration Page 33, paragraph 3. The five most important issues were crime, drugs, war, terrorism, racism and health

Q50. A – True Page 33, paragraph 3

UK TODAY: A PROFILE

Q1. D – 60 million people Page 35, Table

Q2. A – In 2005, the population in England was 50.1 million, Scotland 5.1 million, Wales 2.9 million and Northern Ireland 1.7m. Page 35, Table

Q3. B – False Page 36, paragraph 1. A census is done every 10 years

Q4. B -2011 Page 36, paragraph 1

Q5. B – A census is a count of the total population Page 35, paragraph 4

Q6. B – Both the birth rate and death rate in the UK is falling Page 35, paragraph 3

Q7. C – to all UK households Page 36, paragraph 2

Q8. B False Page 36, paragraph 2. The form must be completed by law

Q9. B – Ethnic minority groups make up 8.3% of the population Page 36, paragraph 4

Q10. B – False Page 35, paragraph 5. Large numbers have arrived

Q11. A – England Page 37, paragraph 1

Q12. C – 45% Page 37, paragraph 1

Q13. B – One-third Page 37, paragraph 1

Q14. B – Indian Page 36, Table

Q15. C – North East Page 37, paragraph 1

Q16. D – 870 miles Page 37, paragraph 2

Q17. B – English is one of the many languages spoken in the UK Page 37, paragraph 3

Q18. D - London, Liverpool and Tyneside Page 37, paragraph 3

Q19. A – Welsh is spoken in Wales, Gaelic in Scotland and Irish Gaelic in Northern Ireland Page 37, paragraph 4

Q20. A – True Page 37, paragraph 2

Q21. C – 70% Page 38, Table

Q22. B -15% Page 38, Table

Q23. B – King or Queen Page 39, paragraph 1

Q24. B – The Monarch is only allowed to marry a Protestant Page 39, paragraph 1

Q25. B - The Church of England is the official church in England, the Presbyterian Church is the official church in Scotland and Wales and Northern Ireland have no official church Page 39, paragraph 1

Q26. B – 10% Page 38, paragraph 1

Q27. C – Christian, Muslim, Hindu, Sikh, Jewish and Buddhist Page 38, Table

Q28. A – True Page 39, paragraph 2

Q29. B – In the UK, 10% of Christians are Roman Catholic (40% in Northern Ireland) Page 39, paragraph 2

Q30. B – False Page 39, paragraph 4. Bank holidays have no religious or national significance

Q31. C – 23 April (St George's day) Page 39, Table

Q32. A – 1 March (ST David's day) Page 39, Table

Q33. D – 30 November (St Andrew's day) Page 39, Table

Q34. B – 17 March (St Patrick's Day) Page 39, Table

Q35. D – December 26 Page 40, paragraph 2

Q36. A – True Page 40, paragraph 3. 2 January is also a public holiday in Scotland

Q37. A – Customs and traditions from various religions are celebrated in the UK Page 40, paragraph 1

Q38. B – False Page 40, paragraph 2. Only Christmas and Easter are religious holidays

Q39. A – Eid ul-fitr, Diwali and Hanukkah are Muslim, Hindu and Jewish religious festivals. Page 40, paragraph 1

Q40. B – False Page 40, paragraph 4. Valentine's Day fall on February 14

Q41. D – 31 October Page 41, paragraph 1

Q42. B - 5 November Page 41, paragraph 2

Q43. B – Remembrance Day commemorates those who died fighting in the First and second world wars, and other wars Page 41, paragraph 3

Q44. A – Remembrance Day is 11 November and is when many people wear poppies in memory of those who died from wars Page 41, paragraph 3

Q45. B – There is no United Kingdom team for Rugby and football Page 41, paragraph 4. Each home country has their own team

Q46. C – Rugby, cricket, tennis and football Page 41, paragraph 4

Q47. B – False Page 37, paragraph 2. Most of the population live in town and cities

Q48. B – False Page 35, paragraph 2. The population of the UK has grown by 7.7% since 1971

Q49. A – Church of England, D – Anglican Church Page 39, paragraph 1

Q50. C – The Archbishop of Canterbury Page 39, paragraph 1

HOW THE UNITED KINGDOM IS GOVERNED

Q1. D - Parliamentary democracy Page 44, paragraph 3. Also described as constitutional democracy

Q2. A – The UK has a constitutional monarchy Page 43, paragraph 3

Q3. B – False Page 43, paragraph 3. The Queen is the head of state

Q4. B – The King or Queen Page 43, paragraph 3

Q5. B – The United Kingdom has never had a lasting revolution, like America and France Page 43, paragraph 2

Q6. B – The British constitution is not written down in a single document Page 43, paragraph 2

Q7. C – Five years Page 44, paragraph 3; Page 44, paragraph 8

Q8. A –True Page 44, paragraph 8

Q9. B – Members of the House of Commons are all elected Page 44, paragraph 6

Q10. B – False Page 45, paragraph 5. 10 Downing Street is the official home of the Prime minister

Q11. C – 646 Page 44, paragraph 3

Q12. D – Members of the European Parliament Page 45, paragraph 1

Q13. D – The House Secretary Page 45, paragraph 6

Q14. A – The Opposition Page 46, paragraph 2

Q15. C – MPs from the second largest party in the House of Commons Page 46, paragraph 2. There are no MPs in the House of Lords, but peers

Q16. B – False Page 46, paragraph 4. Anyone can stand, but unlikely to win

Q17. B – Prime minister's questions takes place every week Page 46, paragraph 2

Q18. D - The Speaker Page 46, paragraph 3

Q19. B – The Whips are MPs appointed by their party leaders and are responsible for discipline in their party and making sure MPs attend the House of Commons to vote Page 44, paragraph 9

Q20. A – True Page 46, paragraph 4

Q21. B – Managers and administrators who carry out government policy Page 47, paragraph 2

Q22. B – A system where the candidate that gets the most votes in a constituency is elected an MP Page 44, paragraph 8

Q23. B – Chancellor of the Exchequer Page 45, paragraph 6

Q24. A - The Cabinet Secretary; C – The Permanent Secretary Page 45, paragraph 6

Q25. B – There are two parliaments in the United Kingdom Page 47, paragraph 6. The Scottish parliament (Edinburgh) and national parliaments (London)

Q26. B – Wales and C – Northern Ireland Page 47, paragraph 5 and page 48, paragraph 1

Q27. B – Taxation and D – Defence Page 47, paragraph 3

Q28. B – The British National Party Page 46, paragraph 4

Q29. A – The Welsh Assembly, Scottish Parliament and Northern Irish Assembly have 60 members, 129 members and 108 members respectively Page 47, paragraphs 5 and 7, page 48, paragraph 2

Q30. B – False Page 47, paragraph 4 and page 44, paragraph 7. Proportional representation is used in Welsh Assembly and Scottish Parliament, but not in House of Commons.

Q31. B – Defence and D – Social Security Page 48, paragraph 4

Q32. D – Every year in May Page 48, paragraph 6

Q33. C – Car Page 48, paragraph 6

Q34. D – A jury Page 48, paragraph 8

Q35. B – A judge Page 48, paragraph 8

Q36 B – False Page 48, paragraph 7. Judge can ask parliament to consider changing the law

Q37. A – True Page 48, paragraph 7

Q38. A – The police in the UK is organised locally and cannot be instructed by the government on what to do Page 49, paragraph 1

Q39. C – A Non-departmental body Page 49, paragraph 2. Quango also stands for quasi-autonomous national governmental organisation

Q40. B – False Page 49, paragraph 3. The UK has a free press

Q41. C – Law and is must be balanced between parties Page 49, paragraph 5

Q42. A – Broadcasters are Free to interview politicians in a tough manner Page 49, paragraph 5

Q43. A -You must be 18 to vote and majority of UK-born and naturalized citizens have full civic rights to vote Page 49, paragraph 6

Q44. B - European Union nationals are not allowed to vote in general elections Page 49, paragraph 7

Q45. D –The electoral register Page 49, paragraph 8

Q46. B – False Page 50, paragraph 4. Most citizens of the UK, Irish Republic or the Commonwealth aged 18 or over can stand

Q47 B – False Page 50, paragraph 6. Elected members of parliament have a primary duty to serve and represent their constituents

Q48. B – Turning up on the day and D – Getting tickets from a member Page 50, paragraph 7

Q49. A – The King or Queen Page 52, paragraph 2

Q50. A – 53 member states Page 52, paragraph 2

Q51. C – 27 member countries Page 52, paragraph 3

Q52. B – The European Flag and C – The Euro Page 52, paragraph 3, Page 53, paragraph 2

Q52. C – The Council of Europe Page 53, paragraph 4. The Council of Europe was created in 1949 with UK as a founding member.

Q53. B – False Page 52, paragraph 4. Citizens of some of the recent joiners may be restricted or restrictions on grounds of public health, public order and public security is possible

Q53. A – True Page 53, paragraph 3

Q54. D – 5 years Page 53, paragraph 2

Q55. D – The European Commission Page 53, paragraph 1

Q56. B – The Council of Europe Page 53, paragraph 4

Q57. A - All member states of the Council of Europe are bound by the European Convention of Human rights Page 53, paragraph 4

Q58.D – 190 member countries Page 53, paragraph 5

Q59. A – True Page 53, paragraph 5

Q60. A – Convention on Human Rights Page 53, paragraph 6 .The Universal Declaration of human rights applies here

EVERYDAY NEEDS

Q1. B - 2 in 3 Page 55, paragraph 1

Q2. C - Using a Mortgage, which is a special bank loan Page 55, paragraph 2

Q3. B – False Page 55, paragraph 4. Estate agents represent sellers

Q4. C – A solicitor Page 55, paragraph 4. In other countries, it is usually an estate agent

Q5. B – You can make an offer higher than what the seller is asking Page 55, paragraph 5

Q6. B - In some regions of the UK, an offer becomes legally binding earlier than others Page 56, paragraph 1

Q7. B – A solicitor and D – A surveyor Page 56, paragraph 2

Q8. B – False Page 56, paragraph 8

Q9. A – You can rent property from the local authority, housing association or private property owners Page 56, paragraph 3

Q10. A – True Page 56, paragraph 4

Q11. D – Housing associations Page 56, paragraph 7

Q12. B – Lease and C – Tenancy agreement Page 56, paragraph 9

Q13. B – One month's rent Page 57, paragraph 1

Q14. A – True Page 57, paragraph 5

Q15. B – False Page 57, paragraph 6

Q16. C – Local authority Page 57, paragraph 7

Q17. A – True Page 58, paragraph 1

Q18. D – Refuse collection Page 58, paragraph 7

Q19. B - Local government services are paid for partly by Council Tax and central government grants Page 59, paragraph 1

Q20. B – False Page 58, paragraph 7. Waste is normally put outside, in a particular place to get collected

Q21. C – The size and value of the property Page 59, paragraph 1

Q22. A – A disabled person and C – A single person staying at a property Page 59, paragraph 2. Some on a low income may be able to get Council Tax Benefit

Q23. B – Insure the building Page 59, paragraph 3

Q24. D – Neighbours for an amicable solution Page 59, paragraph 4

Q25. B – Information on how to pay bills is normally found on the back of the bill Page 58, paragraph 6

Q26. B - £5 and C - £50 Page 60, paragraph 1

Q27. C – Republic of Ireland and D – France Page 60, paragraph 2

Q28. B – False Page 60, paragraph 1. Notes issued in Scotland and Northern Ireland is valid everywhere in the UK

Q29. B - Debit cards, credit cards and store cards are different ways of paying for things. Page 60, paragraphs 5 and 6

Q30. B - False Page 60, paragraph 4. You would also need to show an address verification document, like a household bill

Q31. B – Credit Card and D – Store card Page 60, paragraph 6

Q32. D – Insurance companies Page 61, paragraphs 1, 2,3 and 4

Q33. B – Members Page 61, paragraph 3

Q34. B – Car insurance Page 61, paragraph 4

Q35. D - A system which pays benefits to people who do not have enough to live on Page 61, paragraph 5

Q36. D – Foreign student Page 61, paragraph 5

Q37. B – Jobcentre Plus offices and C – Post Office Page 61, paragraph 5. Note: Citizens Advice Bureau is an option, not Citizen Bureau

Q38. B -The National Health Service (NHS) started in 1948 and provides free healthcare to residents Page 62, paragraph 1. Only residents are entitled to free health care

Q39. C – A General Practitioner (GP) Page 62, paragraph 2

Q40. C – Seek advice from the Citizens Advice Bureau Page 63, paragraph 4

Q41. D – GP Page 62, paragraph 3

Q42. A - You should register with a GP as soon as possible after you move to a new area. Page 62, paragraph 7

Q43. B - Free prescriptions are only available to a select group of people Page 63, paragraph 3

Q44. B - You may go directly to a hospital's Accident and Emergency (A&E) in an emergency without a GP's letter Page 62, paragraph 6

Q45. B – You are a working 18 year old and live in England Page 63, paragraph 3

Q46. False Page 63, paragraph 5. NHS direct (Telephone) and NHS direct online (Internet)

Q47 C – 999 and D – 112 Page 65, paragraph 4 under 'Check that you understand'

Q48. D – Using the Yellow Pages Page 64, paragraph 5

Q49. A – True Page 64, paragraph 6

Q50. A – Someone receiving child benefit Page 64, paragraph 7. Child benefit is available to parents with children under a certain age not subject to immigration control

Q51. A – True Page 64, paragraph 8

Q52. D – Pharmacy Page 64, paragraph 8

Q53. B – False Page 64, paragraph 8

Q54. B – Chemist Page 64, paragraph 8

Q55. C –Social Security Office Page 65, paragraphs 2, 3 and 4

Q56. B – False Page 65, paragraph 5. Registration should be within six weeks

Q57. B – False Page 65, paragraph 5. Sometimes, only the mother's name is on the certificate

Q58. C – 5 and 16 Page 66, paragraph 1

Q59. B – The Child's guardian and C – The Child's parent Page 66, paragraph 2

Q60. B - The education system in the UK is different in all the four home countries Page 66, paragraph 3

Q61. C – Primary and Secondary Page 66, paragraph 3

Q62. A – True Page 66, paragraph 1

 Q63. B – Primary stage lasts from 6 to 11 in Wales Page 66, paragraph 3. Primary stage lasts from 5 to 11 in England and Wales, 5 to 12 in Scotland and 4 to 11 in Northern Ireland

Q64. B - These are schools where boys and girls study together in the same classes Page 66, paragraph 8

Q65. C – 16 Page 66, paragraph 3

Q66. B – False Page 66, paragraph 9. Only in state schools, but some items are paid for

Q67. B – Independent schools and D – Public schools Page 67, paragraph 2

Q68. B – Local education authority Page 66, paragraph 9

Q69. B – School uniforms and D – Sportswear Page 66, paragraph 9

Q70. A – True Page 66, paragraph 7

Q71. C – A Grammar school Page 67, paragraph 1

Q72. A – True Page 67, paragraph 2

Q73. A – 8% Page 67, paragraph 2

Q74. B – Scotland Page 67, paragraphs 3 and 4

Q75. A – True Page 67, paragraph 3. National curriculum does not apply in Scotland. Private schools may follow a different curriculum

Q76. A – True Page 67, paragraph 4

Q77. C – Four Page 67, paragraph 5

Q78. B – 7, 11, 14 and 16 Page 67, paragraph 5

Q79. B – In Scotland, a broad curriculum informed by national guidance is used in schools Page 67, paragraph 4

Q80. C – 16 and 18 Page 67, paragraph 5

Q81. D – Wales Page 67, paragraph 6

Q82. B – Scotland Page 67, paragraph 7

Q83. D – Standard Grade Page 67, paragraph 7

Q84. C – Six Page 67, paragraph 7. The phases are from A to F

Q85. A – 190 Page 68, paragraph 4

Q86. B - The Governing body of a school decides how the a school is run and administered Page 68, paragraph 3

Q87. C – The local education authority and D – The governing body Page 68, paragraph 3

Q88. C – The School Board Page 68, paragraph 3

Q89. B – At 16, young people decide whether to go for A levels or leave school Page 68, paragraph 5

Q90. A – True Page 68, paragraph 6

Q91. D – English for speakers of other languages Page 68, paragraph 6

Q92. A - Financial assistance (Education Maintenance Allowance) is available to young people from low income families up till age 19 Page 68, paragraph 5

Q93. A – Medical training Page 68, paragraph 6

Q94. D – Any age above 18 Page 68, paragraph 8

Q95. D - £3000 Page 68, paragraph 9

Q96. C – Scotland Page 68, paragraph 9

Q97. B – Students do not have to pay anything before or during studies, but after leaving university Page 69, paragraph 1

Q98. A – True Page 69, paragraph 1

Q99. C – Low interest student loan Page 69, paragraph 1

Q100. C – 14 Page 67, paragraph 9

Q101. B – False Page 69, paragraph 3

Q102. B – 18R Page 69, paragraph 4. R18 is the correct classification for no under 18's allowed, not 18R

Q103. B – A film classified as 12A may be seen or rented by someone under the age of 12 if they are with an adult. Page 69, paragraph 4

Q104. A - Someone watching colour television aged 75 years and B -Someone watching television from DVD players only Page 70, paragraph 1

Q105. D – 12 months Page 70, paragraph 2

Q106. A - Blind people can receive a 50% discount on their TV licence Page 70, paragraph 2

Q107. A - Watching TV without a licence is a criminal offence Page 70, paragraph 2

Q108. B -The National Trust is a charity that works to preserve important buildings and countryside in the UK Page 70, paragraph 4

Q109. C – 18 Page 70, paragraph 5

Q110. A – True Page 70, paragraph 5

Q111. C – 18 Page 70, paragraph 7

Q112. A – 16 Page 70, paragraph 7

Q113. A – True Page 70, paragraph 8

Q114. A – Cats and D – Dogs Page 70, paragraph 8

Q115. A - It is against British law to treat pets cruelly Page 70, paragraph 8

Q116. D – National rail Page 71, paragraph 1

Q117. D – Secretaries Page 71, paragraph 2

Q118. A – All taxes and minicabs must be licensed to operate lawfully Page 71, paragraph 3

Q119. D – 21 Page 71, paragraph 4

Q120. A -17 Page 71, paragraph 4

Q121. B – 18 Page 71, paragraph 4

Q122. A – True Page 71, paragraph 5

Q123. B - You are required to pass a theory and practical test in order to get a full driving licence. Page 71, paragraph 6

Q124. D - Apply for provisional licence, pass theory test, then pass practical test Page 71, paragraph 6

Q125. B - Once you get a licence, it can be used until the age of 70 upon which it is renewed every three years Page 71, paragraph 7

Q126. B – 12 months Page 72, paragraph 1

Q127. A – True Page 71, paragraph 9

Q128. A - It is a criminal offence to drive a car without proper motor insurance Page 72, paragraph 2

Q129. A – 3 year old Page 72, paragraph 4

Q130. B – The post office Page 72, paragraph 3

Q131. B - An MOT certificate is compulsory, and not having one is an offence and invalidates your auto insurance. Page 72, paragraph 4

Q132. B - Everyone in a vehicle should wear seat belts Page 72, paragraph 5

Q133. D – Sikh men wearing a turban Page 72, paragraph 5

Q134. A – True Page 72, paragraph 5

Q135. B – False Page 72, paragraph 6

Q136. D – A driver having more than the permitted amount of alcohol Page 72, paragraph 6

Q137. D – A breathalyser test Page 72, paragraph 6

Q138. B - 30 mph in built-up areas, 60 mph on single carriageways and 70 mph on motorways Page 72, paragraph 6

Q139. A – True Page 72, paragraph 6

Q140. C -112 and D – 999 Page 72, paragraph 7

Q141. A – True Page 72, paragraph 7

Q142 B – False Page 73, paragraph 1. The insurance company may refuse to pay if you admit fault

Q143. A - If involved in an accident, exchange names, addresses, vehicle registration numbers and insurance details with the other driver Page 72, paragraph 7

Q144. B – False Page 73, paragraph 2

Q145. B – A National Insurance number card and C – A provisional driving licence Page 73, paragraph 3

EMPLOYMENT

Q1. B - False Page 75, paragraph 1. Some people need work permits

Q2. C – Local Bank Page 75, paragraph 2

Q3. A – National Academic Recognition Information Centre Page 75, paragraph 4

Q4. C – NARIC Page 75, paragraph 4

Q5. B – Jobcentre Plus Page 75, paragraph 3

Q6. A – True Page 76, paragraph 2

Q7. B - A referee for a job application should be someone who is not a family member or personal friend Page 76, paragraph 4

Q8. B – False Page 76, paragraph 6. You could be dismissed if a job was obtained on false information

Q9. A - A criminal record check is also called a Criminal Records Bureau check Page 76, paragraph 7

Q10. D – Department for Work and Pensions Page 76, paragraph 8

Q11. A – True Page 76, paragraph 9

Q12. B – False Page 77, paragraph 1

Q13. C – Working in someone's home Page 77, paragraph 4

Q14. A – True Page 77, paragraph 1

Q15. B – The Equal opportunities commission and age discrimination Page 77, paragraph 5 and Page 78, paragraph 1

Q16. C – Commission for Equality and Human Rights Page 78, paragraph 1

Q17. A – The Equality Commission Page 78, paragraph 2

Q18. B – False Page 78, paragraph 8

Q19. A - Employers are responsible for the behaviour of their employees while they are at work Page 78, paragraph 8

Q20. B – Citizens Advice Bureau and C – Equal Opportunities Commission Page 78, paragraph 8

Q21. C – Comments about your performance at work Page 78, paragraph 7

Q22. A - Employers and employees both have legal responsibilities at work Page 79, paragraph 1

Q23 B – Two months Page 79, paragraph 2

Q24. A - The contract or written statement is useful in solving disputes between employer and employee Page 79, paragraph 2

Q25. D - £5.35 Page 79, paragraph 4

Q26. B - £4.45 Page 79, paragraph 4

Q27. D - £3.30 Page 79, paragraph 4

Q28. B - It is up to an employee to agree to work more hours than agreed on a contract Page 79, paragraph 6

Q29. A – Tax payment and D – National Insurance payments Page 79, paragraph 7

Q30. A – True Page 79, paragraph 5

Q31. C – Four weeks Page 79, paragraph 7

Q32. D – HM Revenue and Customs Page 79, paragraph 8

Q33. A – True Page 79, paragraph 8

Q34. A – True Page 79, paragraph 8

Q35. A – State Retirement Pensions Page 80, paragraph 1

Q36. B – Child Benefit Page 80, paragraph 1. Child benefit is not means tested

Q37. A - Local Social Security Office and B – Jobcentre Plus Page 80, paragraph 4

Q38. A – True Page 80, paragraph 1

Q39. B - State Pension age for men is 65 and for women is currently 60 years Page 80, paragraph 5

Q40. A – 65 years Page 80, paragraph 5

Q41. C – The Pension Service Page 80, paragraph 5

Q42. A - In addition to a State Pensions, occupational pension schemes and personal pension schemes also exist Page 80, paragraph 6

Q43. B – False Page 80, paragraph 6. The Pensions Advisory Service is different from the State Pensions Service

Q44. A – Your bank manager Page 81, paragraph 3

Q45. B - A trade union is an organisation that aims to improve the pay and working conditions of their members Page 81, paragraph 1

Q46. D – Trades Union Congress Page 81, paragraph 1

Q47. B – The national Advisory, Conciliation and Arbitration Service (ACAS) Page 81, paragraph 3

Q48. A. An employee can be dismissed immediately for serious misconduct at work Page 81, paragraph 4

Q49. A – True Page 81, paragraph 5

Q50. C – Requesting a pay increase Page 81, paragraph 4

Q51. A – 3 months Page 81, paragraph 5

Q52. B – Jobseekers allowance Page 81, paragraph 8

Q53. D – Employment Tribunal Page 81, paragraph 5

Q54. B – Job loss resulting from the closure of a business unit and C – Job loss resulting from the company unable to afford payments Page 81, paragraph 7

Q55. A - The amount of redundancy pay received is dependent on length of time of employment Page 81, paragraph 7

Q56. A - Self-employed people are responsible for paying their own tax and National Insurance Page 82, paragraph 4

Q57. D – An accountant Page 82, paragraph 4

Q58. A – A bank and B – Business Link Page 82, paragraph 6

Q59. B – False Page 82, paragraph 4. Records are to be sent every year

Q60. B – False Page 82, paragraph 7

Q61. B – False Page 84, paragraphs 1 and 2

Q62. C – 26 weeks Page 84, paragraph 1

Q63. A - Fathers are entitled to two weeks paid paternity leave when their child is born, provided they have worked for a company for 26 weeks Page 84, paragraph 2

Q64. B - Maternity leave is available to both part-time and full time working women Page 84, paragraph 1

Q65. B - Some women on maternity leave are paid for the period they are on leave Page 84, paragraph 1

Q66. B – 14 years Page 84, paragraph 5

Q67. B – Newspaper delivery and C – Working in a supermarket Page 84, paragraph 6

Q68. A – True Page 84, paragraph 5

Q69. A - They must not work before 8a.m. or after 8p.m. Page 84, paragraph 7. They must not work before 7a.m. or after 7p.m.

Q70. A - Children aged 14-16 years should not work for more than 4 hours without a one-hour rest break Page 84, paragraph 7

Q71. B - Children who work need both an employment card from their local authority and a medical certificate of fitness for work Page 84, paragraph 6

Q72. B – The Local Authority Page 85, paragraph 1

Q73. A – True Page 84, paragraph 4

Q74. D – The unemployed Page 82, paragraph 1

Q75. B - Children under the age of 14 may be allowed to do some work provided a licence is received from the local authority Page 84, paragraph 5. Specific work in performing, modelling, sport and agriculture may be allowed with a licence from the local authority